Social Studies Crossword Puzzles

AND MORE

Grades 1–4

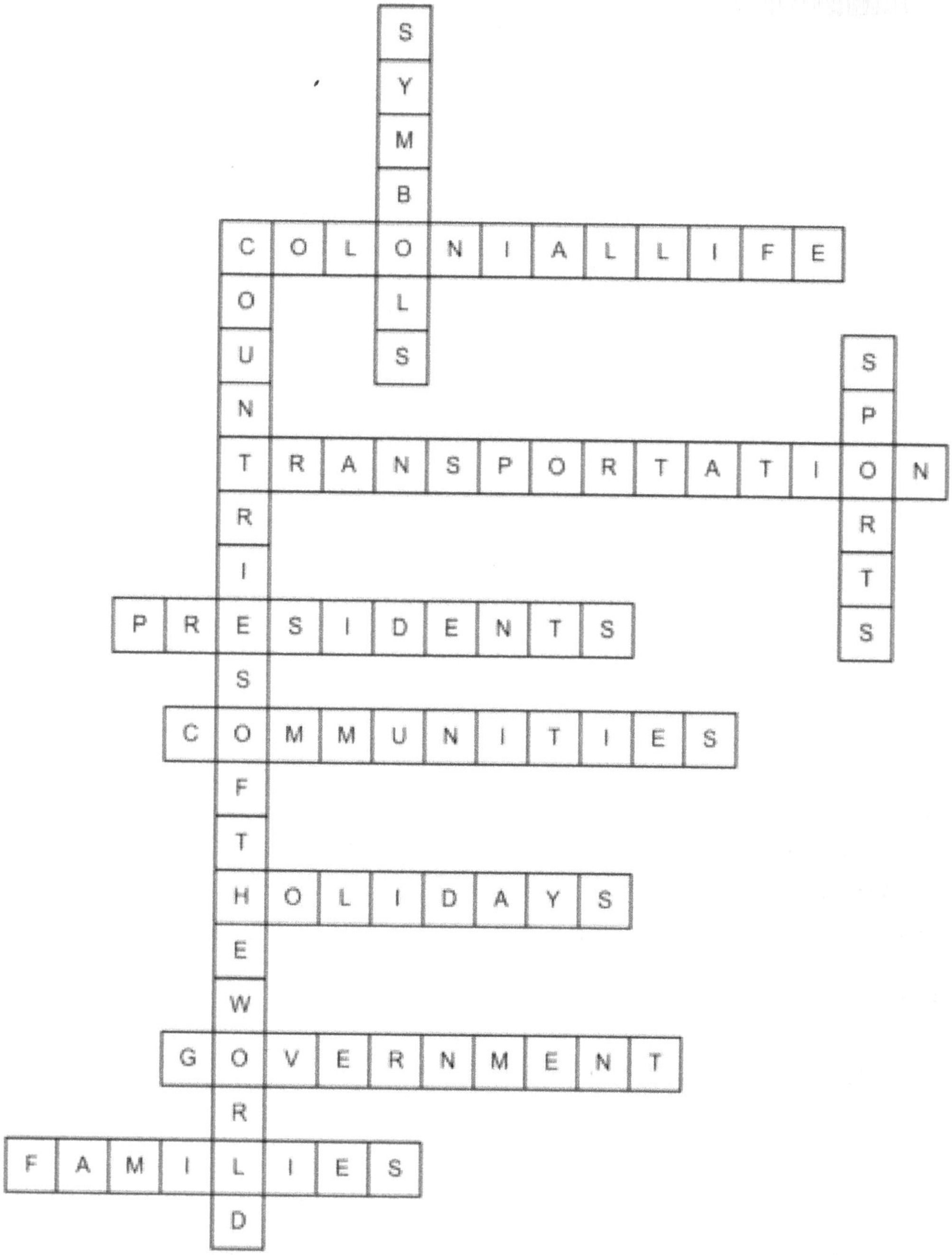
SYMBOLS
COLONIALLIFE
COUNTRIESOFTHEWORLD
SPORTS
TRANSPORTATION
PRESIDENTS
COMMUNITIES
HOLIDAYS
GOVERNMENT
FAMILIES

Written by Rebecca Stark

ISBN 978-1-54466-568-9

EDUCATIONAL BOOKS 'N' BINGO

Printed in the United States of America.

TABLE OF CONTENTS

*An alphabetical list of possible answers from which to choose is provided for each crossword puzzle. Use these lists at your discretion.

Countries of the World

ACROSS

2   Country where Eiffel Tower is found

6   The only country that is also a continent

9   Its capital city is London

10 Largest country in South America

11 Its capital is Berlin

13 Rome, Florence, and Milan are important cities

DOWN

1   Lions and elephants are native to this country in East Africa

3   Largest country; Important cities are Moscow and St. Petersburg

4   African nation famous for its pyramids

5   Forms northern border of the United States

6   Its capital is Buenos Aires

7   Capital city is Beijing

8   Tokyo is the capital and largest city

12 Spanish-speaking nation of North America

Countries of the World

© Barbara M. Peller   Social Studies Crossword Puzzles: Grades 1–4

Communities

ACROSS

3   Person you see when you are sick

6   Where people go to deposit money

7   A place where people get medical treatment

10 Where a family might go to eat a meal

11 Bats, balls and mitts are needed for this sport

12 What a postal worker delivers

13 ___ officers help keep us safe

14 Person who examines your teeth

DOWN

1   Brownies and cubs are two types

2   People go to churches, synagogues, and mosques to do this

4   The leader of a classroom

5   Where you go to borrow a book

8   Where groceries are sold

9   A veterinarian's patients

15 Where you go to learn

 Science Crossword Puzzles: Grades 6 & Up

Communities

7   Social Studies Crossword Puzzles: Grades 1–4

Families

ACROSS

5   Your mother's or father's mother

6   Your mother and father

8   What many children call their father

9   Your mother's or father's sister

10 Your mother's or father's brother

11 Your sister's or brother's son

13 A boy who has the same mother and father as you

DOWN

1   Your aunt's or uncle's child

2   A girl who as the same mother and father as you

3   What many children call their mother

4   Your sister's or brother's daughter

5   Your mother's or father's father

7   A brother or sister

12 Your family's cat or dog

14 Two children born at the same birth

Families

9   Social Studies Crossword Puzzles: Grades 1–4

Government

ACROSS

2   Rules enforced by the government

4   In this system of government the power rests with the people

6   Head of the Executive Branch of our government

7   Branch that comprises the Senate and the House of Representatives

8   The President and vice-president are in this branch

9   A legal member of a country

11   Another name for the legislative branch of our government

12   Branch of government comprising courts and judges

13   Advisors to the President

DOWN

1   Elected head of city or town

3   Document that is the highest law in the land

5   Elected head of a state

8   Process of choosing someone to hold public office by voting

10   Power of the President to reject a bill

14   What a proposed law is called before it is passed

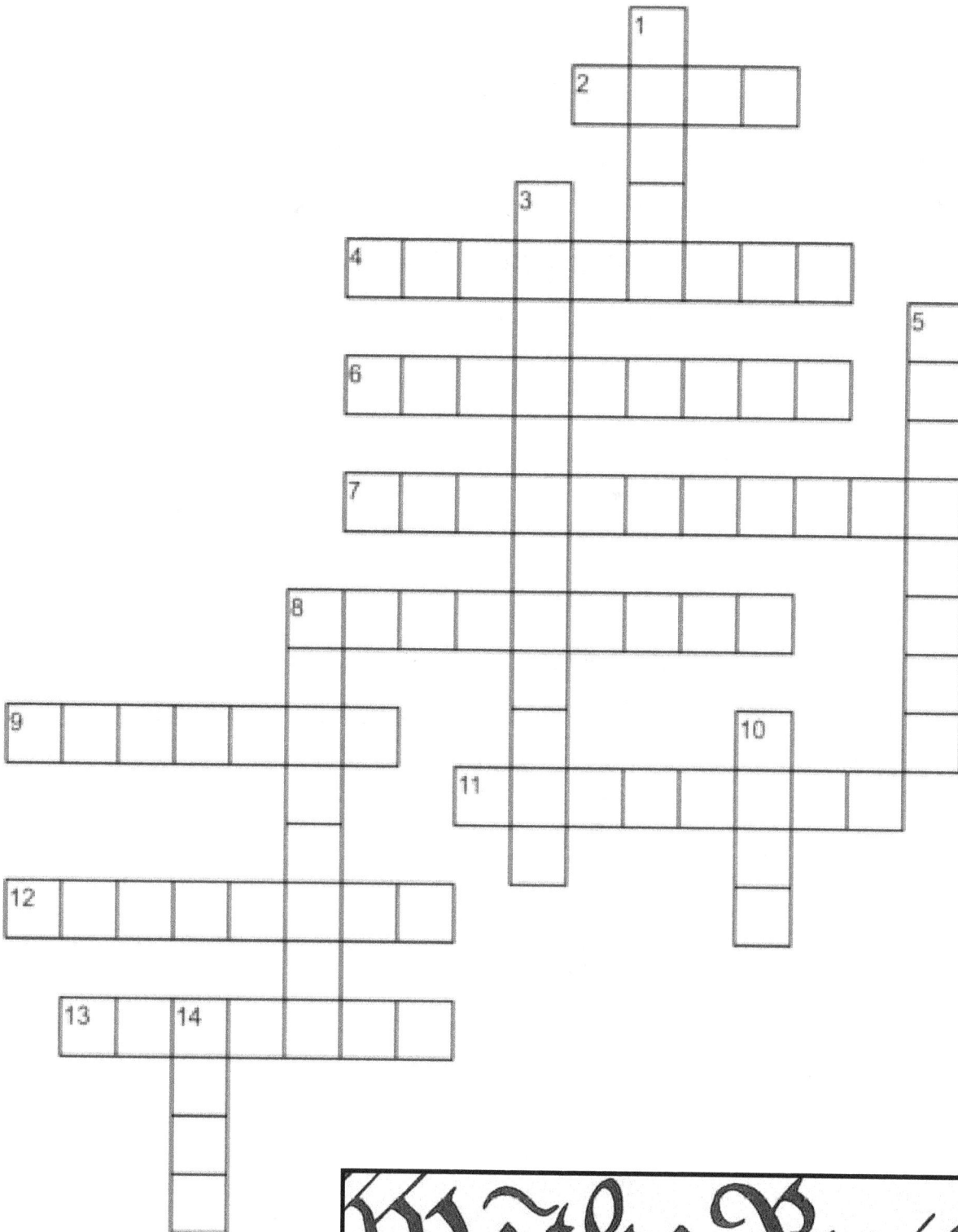

Government

11 Social Studies Crossword Puzzles: Grades 1–4

Holidays and Symbols

ACROSS

2   We celebrate the adoption of our flag in this month

5   Many families eat turkey on this holiday

6   This symbol of American independence is in Philaelphia (2 words)

7   Officially, Presidents' Day celebrates his birthday

8   Children dress up and ask for treats on this holiday

10 On February 14 you might give a card to your ____

DOWN

1   November 11 is a day to honor ____

3   Civil right leader; his birthday is celebrated on the third Monday in February (last name)

4   July 4 is called ____ Day

9   Fathers Day is in June; Mothers Day is in this month

11 On December 31 we celebrate the coming of the ____ ____ (2 words)

12 Annual event celebrated on April 22 (2 words)

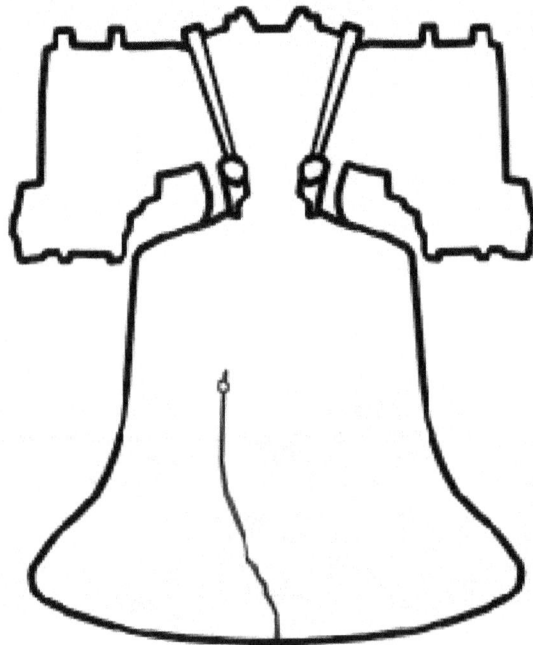

Holidays and Symbols

Presidents

ACROSS

4   Only President to serve 4 terms (Initials)

6   Where President lives (2 words)

7   Third President; wrote most of the Declaration of Independence

10 Wife of a President

11 Branch of government headed by the President

12 First African-American President

13 The President must be a natural born ___ of the United States

DOWN

1   The President is commander-in-chief of the U.S. ___ (2 words)

2   President during the American Civil War

3   President's right to reject a decision or proposal made by Congress

4   Month in which Presidents' Day is celebrated

5   The President must be at least 35 years of ___

6   First President of the United States

8   Number of years in a complete term for the President

9   Fourth President; sometimes called the Father of the Constitution

14 Number of full terms a President can serve

Presidents

Social Studies Crossword Puzzles: Grades 1–4

Sports

ACROSS

1 Players of this sport try to kick or head the ball into the opponents' goal

6 Yearly championship series of Major League Baseball (2 words)

8 Objective is to shoot a ball through a hoop

9 International competition for association football (called soccer in USA); held every 4 years

10 Played on skates; object is to propel a puck past a goal (2 words)

11 Sport in which two teams of six players are separated by a net

DOWN

1 Yearly championship series of National Football League (2 words)

2 Players use head of a stick to carry, pass, catch, and shoot a ball into the goal

3 This is an event in the Summer Olympic Games

4 A racket sport; can be played against a single opponent or in teams of 2

5 Includes athletic contests based on running, jumping, and throwing (3 words)

7 Players use various clubs to hit balls into a series of holes

12 Bat-and-ball game played between two teams of nine players

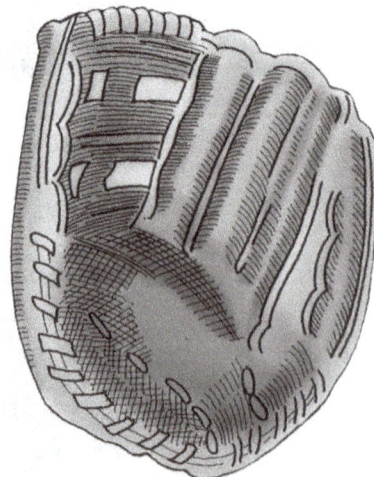

Social Studies Crossword Puzzles: Grades 1–4

Sports

Social Studies Crossword Puzzles: Grades 1–4

Transportation

ACROSS

3   Boats, ferries, and barges

4   A pleasure voyage on a ship

6   Where you go to take a trip on a plane

7   Artificial waterway that allows the passage of boats or ships

9   City with a harbor for seagoing ships

12 A vessel larger than a boat that transports people or goods by sea

DOWN

1   A large motor vehicle carrying passengers by road

2   A large, heavy motor vehicle used for transporting goods

3   Cars, truck, trains, and airplanes

5   Paved land route between two places

8   Short name for an automobile

10 Main types of transportation: water, land, and ___

11 A connected line of railroad cars

Transportation

Colonial Life

ACROSS

3 Large farms in Southern Colonies

5 Declaration of Independence was signed in Independence Hall in this city

6 Founded in 1565 by Spanish explorers (2 words, 1 is abbreviated)

8 Founded by Roger Williams, who wanted religious freedom (2 words}

11 Was capital of the Colonial Virginia

13 Cotton and ___ were 2 important cash crops

14 Native Americans taught settlers how to grow this important food crop

15 Crafted casks that held tobacco, gunpowder, flour and other goods

16 Colonists dressed as Native Americans threw tea into this harbor

DOWN

1 First permanent English settlement; in Virginia

2 Religious group that founded the Massachusetts Bay Colony

4 Named New York in 1664 when English took control of the area (2 words}

7 Sailed on Mayflower and founded Plymouth Colony

9 A druggist; prescribed medicine and provided medical treatment

10 Made and sold fashionable goods; usually a woman

12 He fashioned items from iron and steel in their forge

Colonial Life

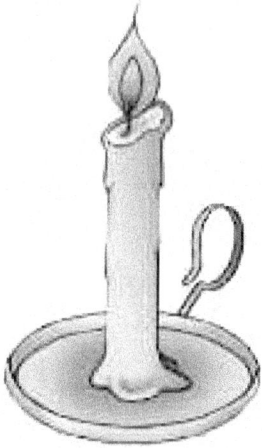

21   Social Studies Crossword Puzzles: Grades 1–4

Mixed Topics

ACROSS

1   What the stars on the flag represent

8   Continent on which the United States is located (2 words)

9   Head of the state government

10 Ocean that borders the continental United States on the east

11 Thomas Edison was one

13 State in which San Francisco is located

15 First person to walk on the moon

16 The first 10 amendments to the Constitution: the Bill of ___

DOWN

2   The Nile River flows through this nation

3   Antonym of "urban"

4   Number of stripes on the American flag

5   What the Fourth of July is called (2 words)

6   Harbor where Statue of Liberty is found (2 words)

7   Ocean that borders the continental United States on the west

12 Continent where China is located

14 Capital and largest city in Massachusetts

Mixed Topics

Career Word Search

```
Q M L O L M L D P U R A P H E V
A V P L X K X L E X V O D V C A
V A Q O U J X J M L L J Q N Q R
J A D F S E O F O I K J O A J E
S U N C J T E I C C Y S R I H T
D V L E E M A E G B B I E R U H
E F W V Z B O L U Q X M K A R G
N Z K F C F E S W R R K A R N I
T B D L F U D E R O W Z B B R F
I H J I M R M J Z E R D J I E E
S K C N I A F C Z N M K I L T R
T E I V U R E Y W A L K E A I I
R Y E F O R R E B R A B K R A F
H R W S M S S E R T I A W Q W W
L D M S J H Y E Z N Q D G P E T
N R O Y A M L A P I C N I R P B
```

BAKER

BARBER

BUS DRIVER

DENTIST

FIREFIGHTER

LAWYER

LIBRARIAN

MAYOR

NURSE

POLICE OFFICER

POSTAL WORKER

PRINCIPAL

TEACHER

WAITER

WAITRESS

Social Studies Crossword Puzzles: Grades 1–4

Nations of the Word Search

```
C U J A P A N M A N S I C
H I N U I J N T E Y V A B
I T H I M S I E U X N W R
N A D Y T S S G L A I E D
A L V N A E E U D I N C K
A Y I D A R D A R I H G O
N I O Z M L G S G O U C T
E H D A A Y G E T C Z O A
D K N N A R R N N A S Z E
E Y W W I I B Y E T T Y H
W P R Q A E G Y P T I E A
S O U T H K O R E A Z N S
N L E O Q V E C N A R F A
```

ARGENTINA

BRAZIL

CANADA

CHILE

CHINA

EGYPT

ENGLAND

FRANCE

GERMANY

INDIA

ITALY

JAPAN

KENYA

MEXICO

NIGERIA

NORWAY

RUSSIA

SOUTH KOREA

SWEDEN

UNITED STATES

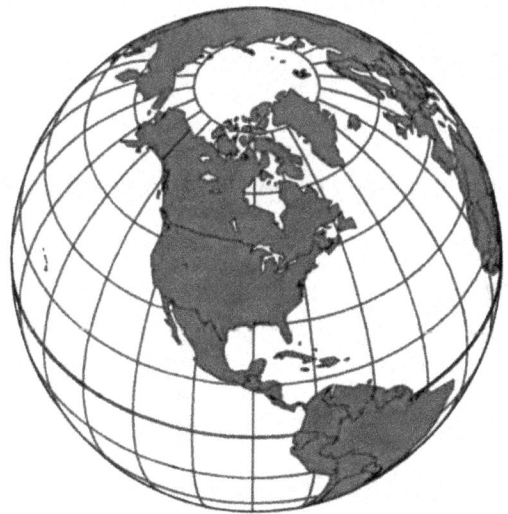

25   Social Studies Crossword Puzzles: Grades 1–4

Anagrams

An anagram is a word, phrase, or name formed by rearranging the letters of another.

Example: POT and TOP

Use the clues to rearrange the letters of the given words to create anagrams.

1. RAW   _____
CLUE: an armed conflict

2. VETO   _____
CLUE: what citizens do to choose a President

3. TASTE   _____
CLUE: California, for example

4. PAINS   _____
CLUE: a nation in Europe

5. MARY   _____
CLUE: an organized military force

6. HIPS   _____
CLUE: a means of transportation

7. MEAT   _____
CLUE: a group of people working together with common goal

8. KALE   _____
CLUE: a large body of water surrounded by land

9. AWL   _____
CLUE: a rule of conduct

10. OILS   _____
CLUE: upper level of earth

Solutions*

*Optional Lists of Answers

Alphabetical lists of the answers are provided. These may be used to help solve the puzzle from the beginning, to assist those having difficulty, or not at all.

Countries of the World

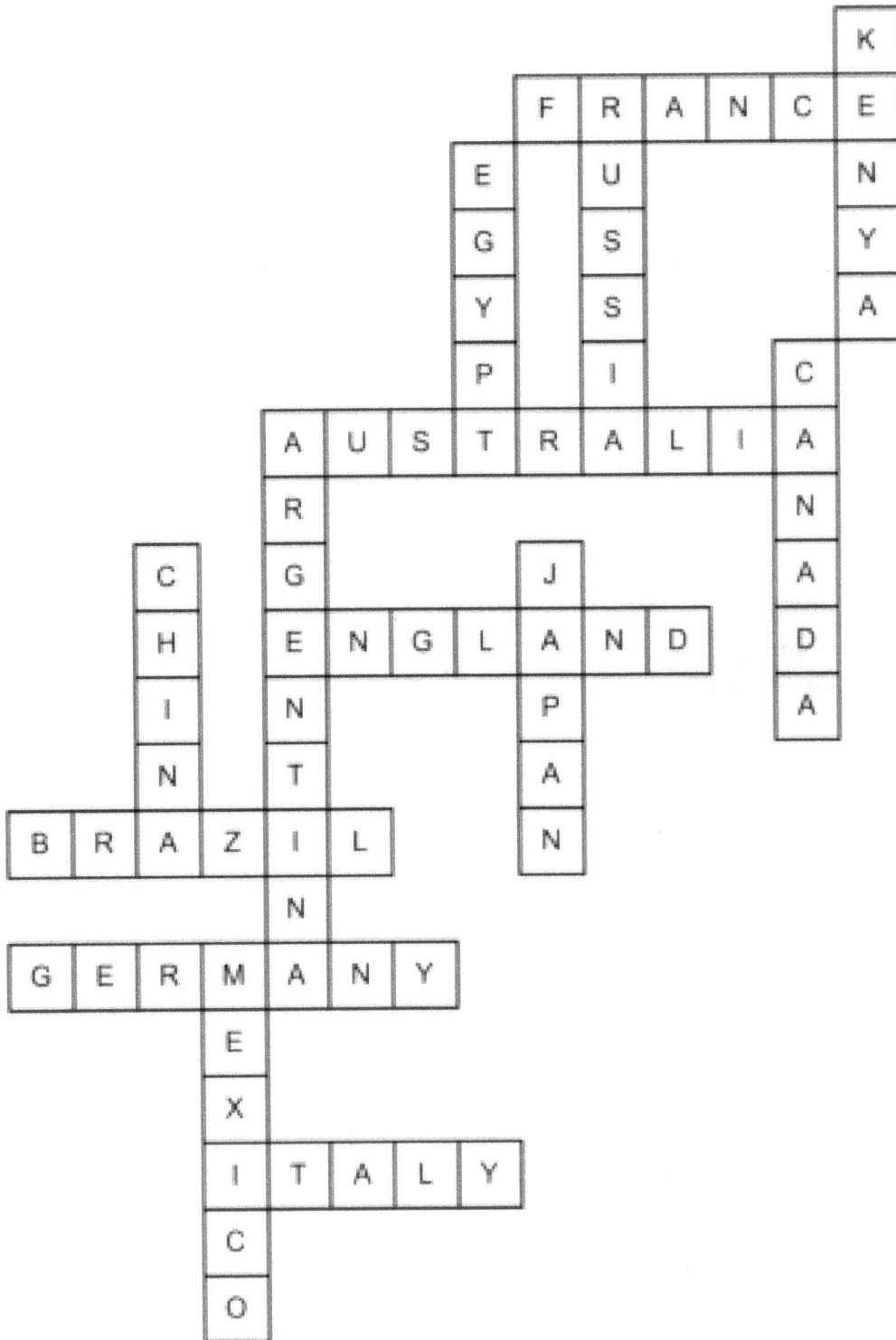

A crossword puzzle with the following answers filled in:

- FRANCE (across)
- KENYA (down)
- RUSSI (down, reads R-U-S-S-I)
- EGYPT (down)
- CANADA (down)
- AUSTRALIA (across)
- ARGENTINA (down)
- CHINA (down)
- ENGLAND (across)
- JAPAN (down)
- BRAZIL (across)
- GERMANY (across)
- MEXICO (down)
- ITALY (across)

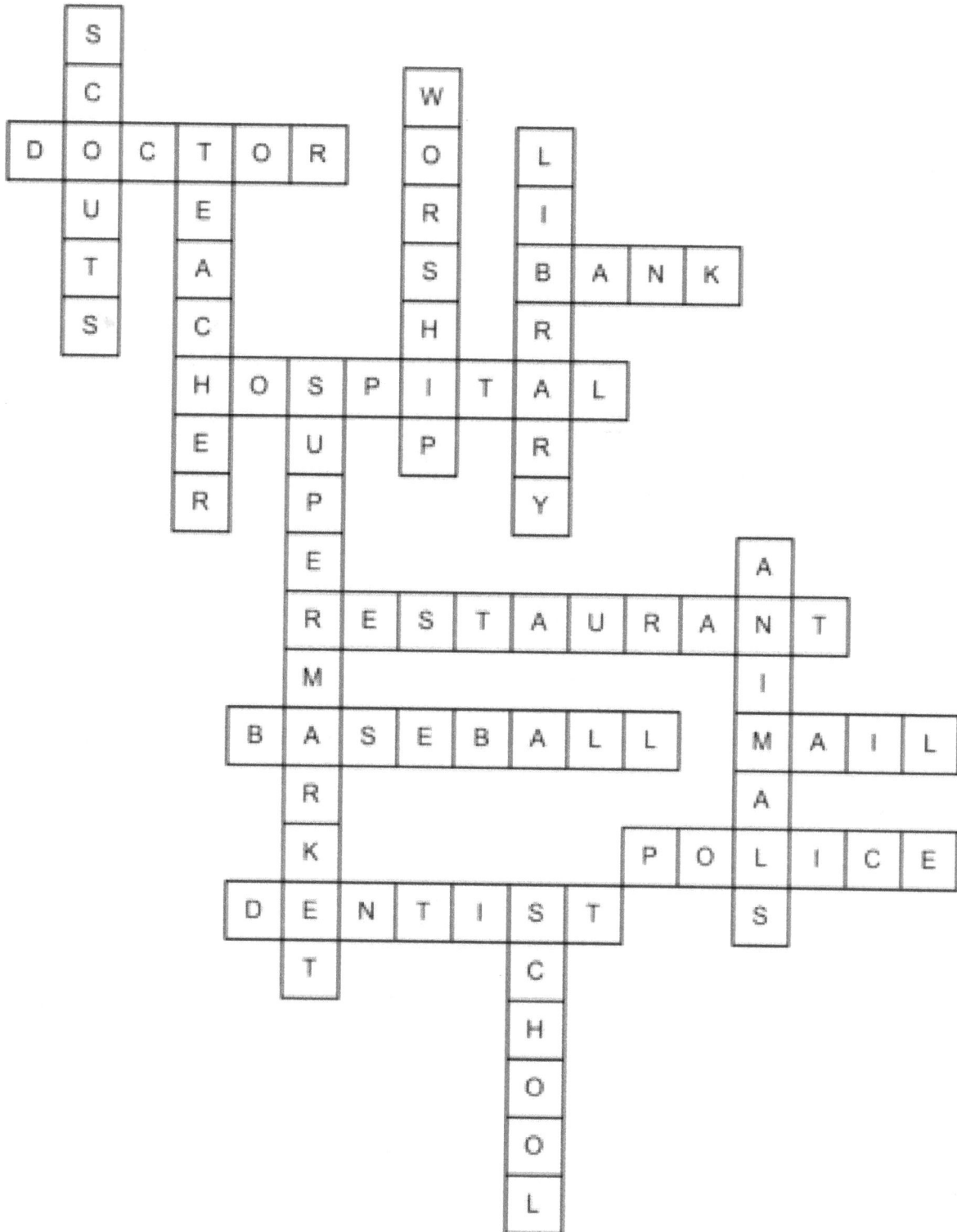

Communities

S
C
D O C T O R
U E
T A
S C
H O S P I T A L
E U
R P

W
O
R L
S I
H B A N K
P R
A
L
R
Y

E
R E S T A U R A N T
M I
B A S E B A L L M A I L
R A
K P O L I C E
D E N T I S T S
T C
H
O
O
L

A

Families

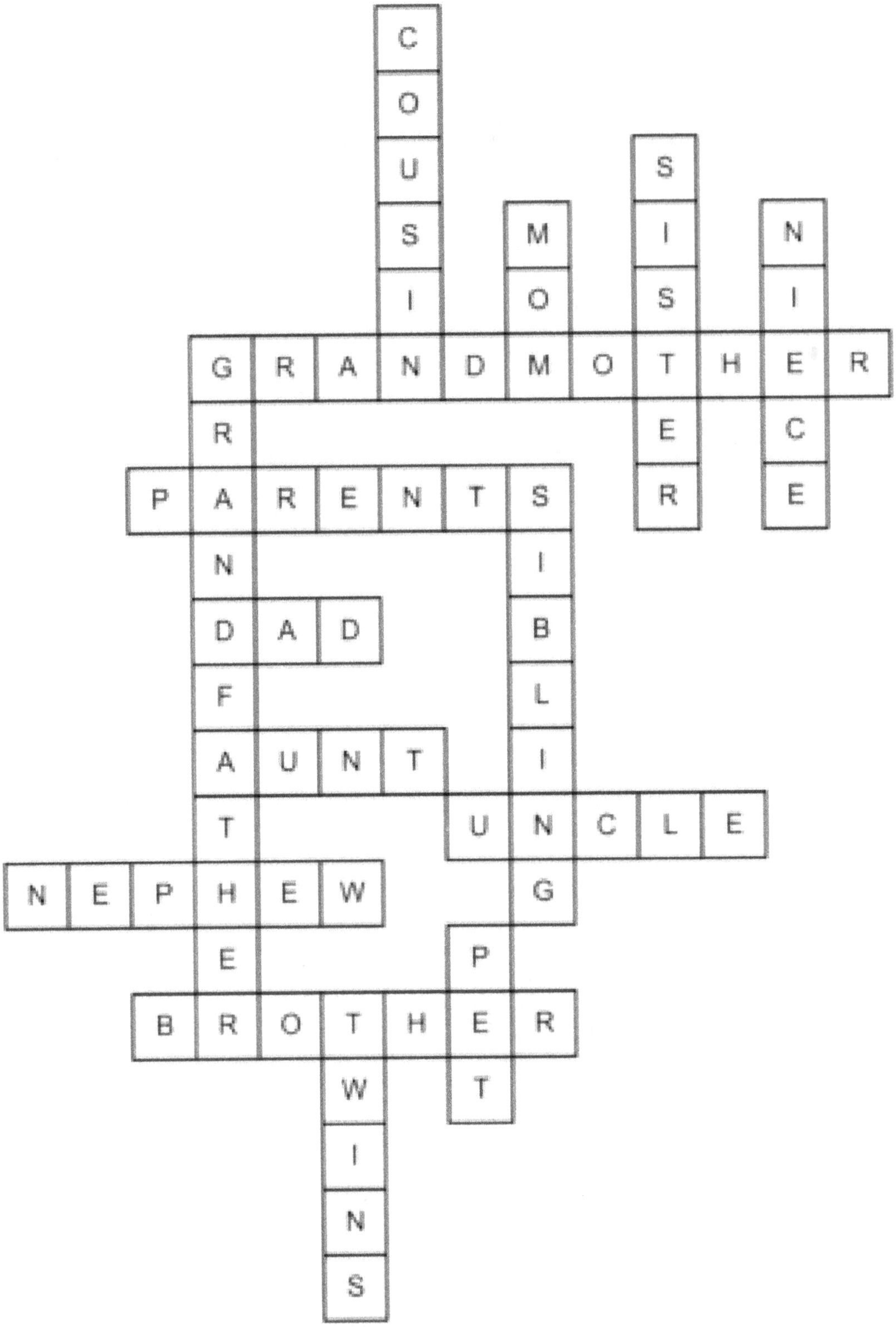
COUSIN
SISTER
MOM
NIECE
GRANDMOTHER
GRANDFATHER
PARENTS
SIBLINGS
DAD
AUNT
UNCLE
NEPHEW
PET
BROTHER
TWINS

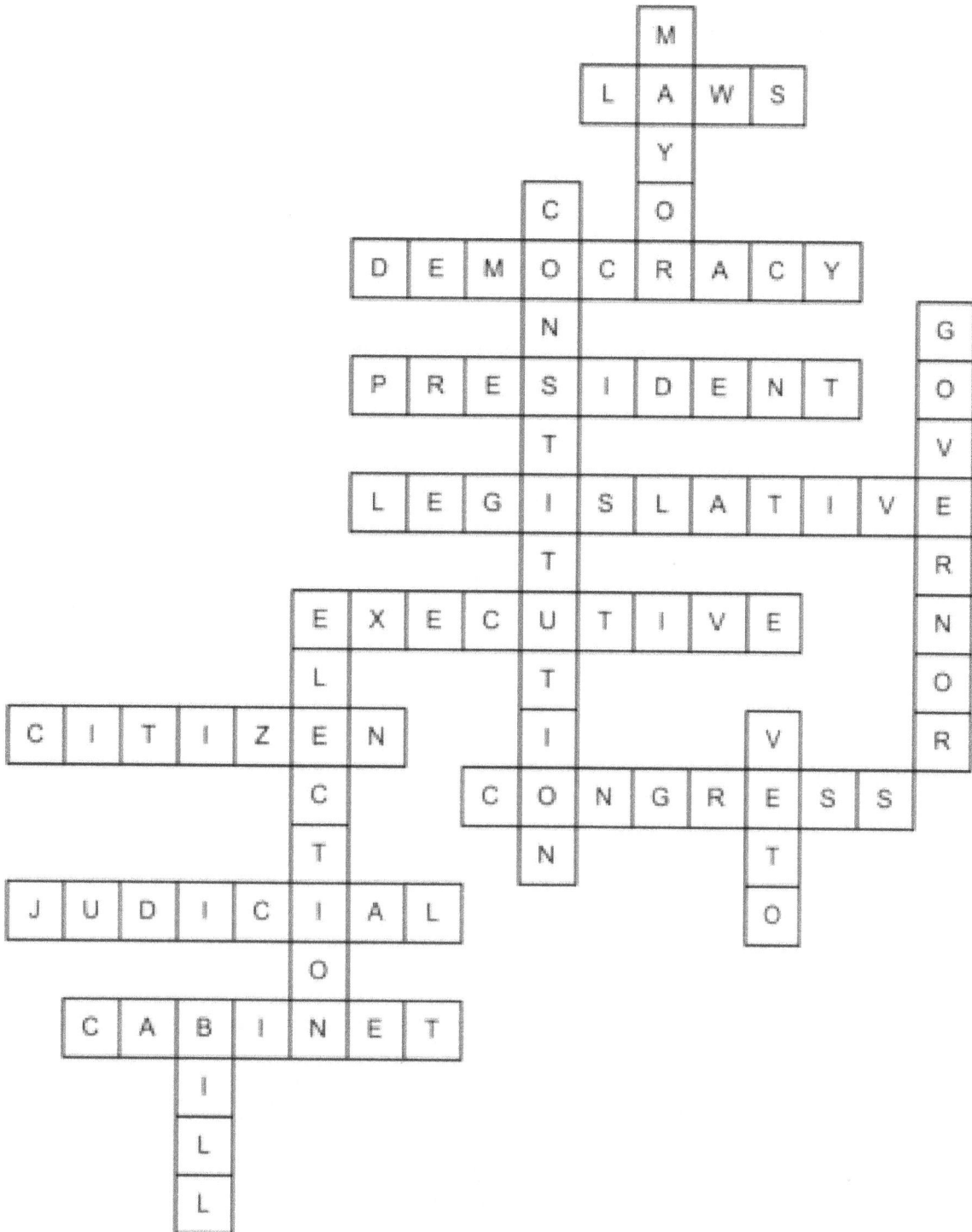

Government

```
                                    M
                           L   A    W   S
                                    Y
                    C               O
        D   E   M   O   C   R   A   C   Y
                    N                              G
        P   R   E   S   I   D   E   N   T          O
                    T                              V
        L   E   G   I   S   L   A   T   I   V   E  E
                    T                              R
            E   X   E   C   U   T   I   V   E      N
            L               T                      O
C   I   T   I   Z   E   N    I              V      R
            C               T              E
            T           C   O   N   G   R   E   S   S
            O           O                  T
J   U   D   I   C   I   A   L              O
            N
    C   A   B   I   N   E   T
            I
            L
            L
```

Holidays and Symbols

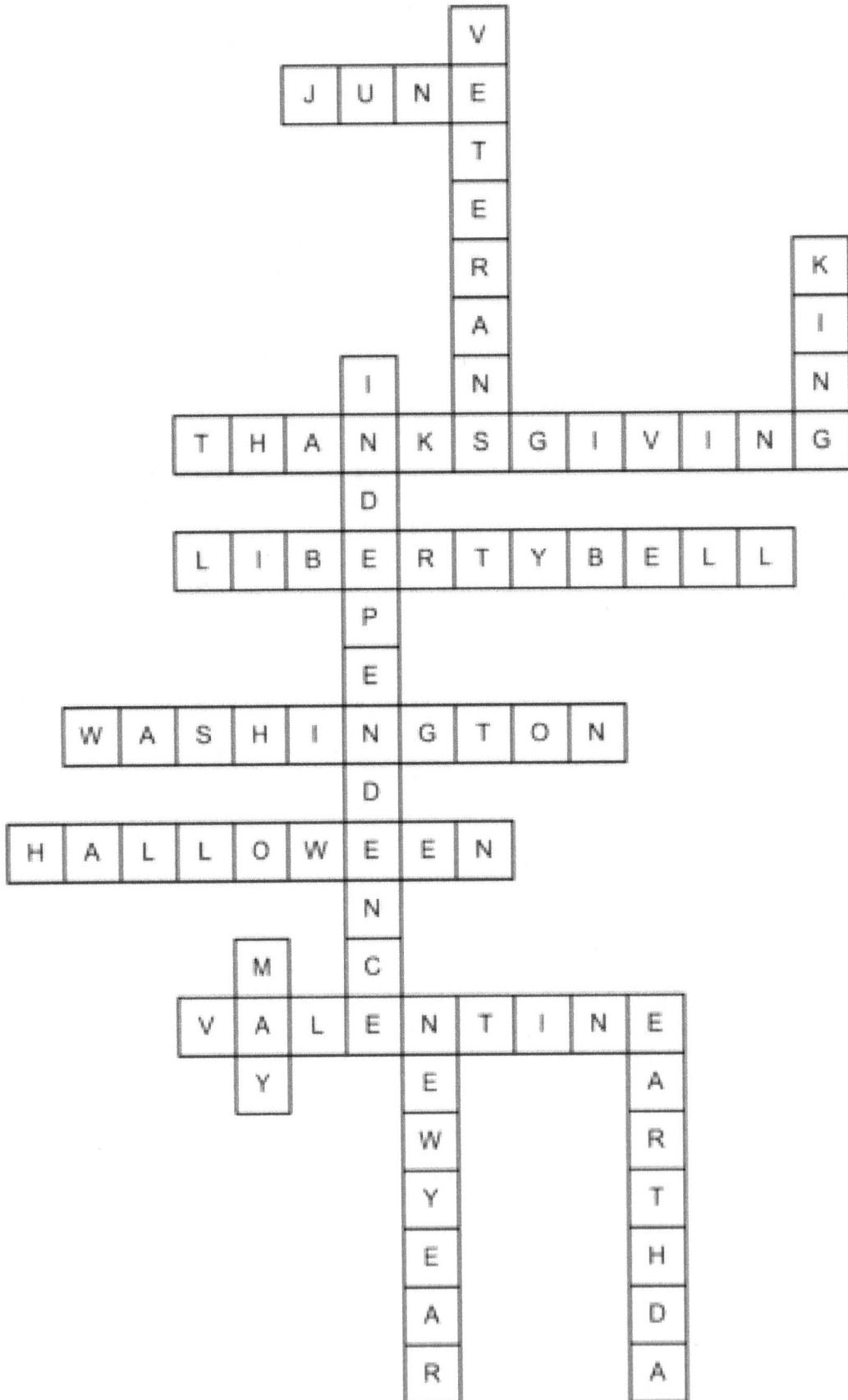

A crossword puzzle with the following answers filled in:

- VETERAN (down, crossing JUNE)
- JUNE (across)
- KING (down)
- THANKSGIVING (across)
- INDEPENDENCE (down)
- LIBERTYBELL (across)
- WASHINGTON (across)
- HALLOWEEN (across)
- MAY (down)
- VALENTINE (across)
- NEWYEAR (down)
- BIRTHDAY (down)

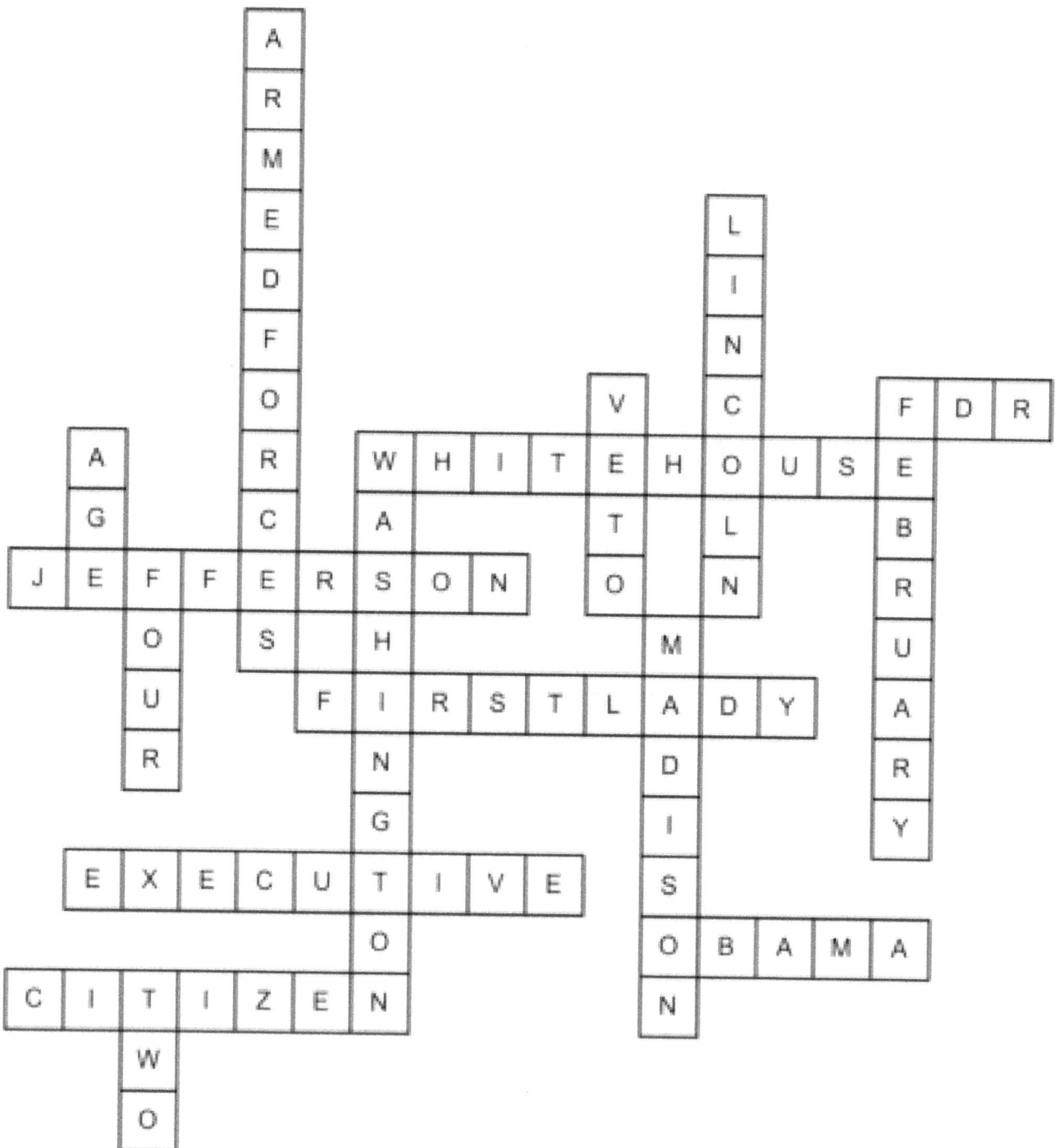

Presidents

ARMEDFORCES (down)

LINCOLN (down)

FDR (across)

WHITEHOUSE (across)

AG (down)

JEFFERSON (across)

VETO (down)

FEBRUARY (down)

FOUR (down)

WASHINGTON (down)

FIRSTLADY (across)

MADISON (down)

EXECUTIVE (across)

OBAMA (across)

CITIZEN (across)

TWO (down)

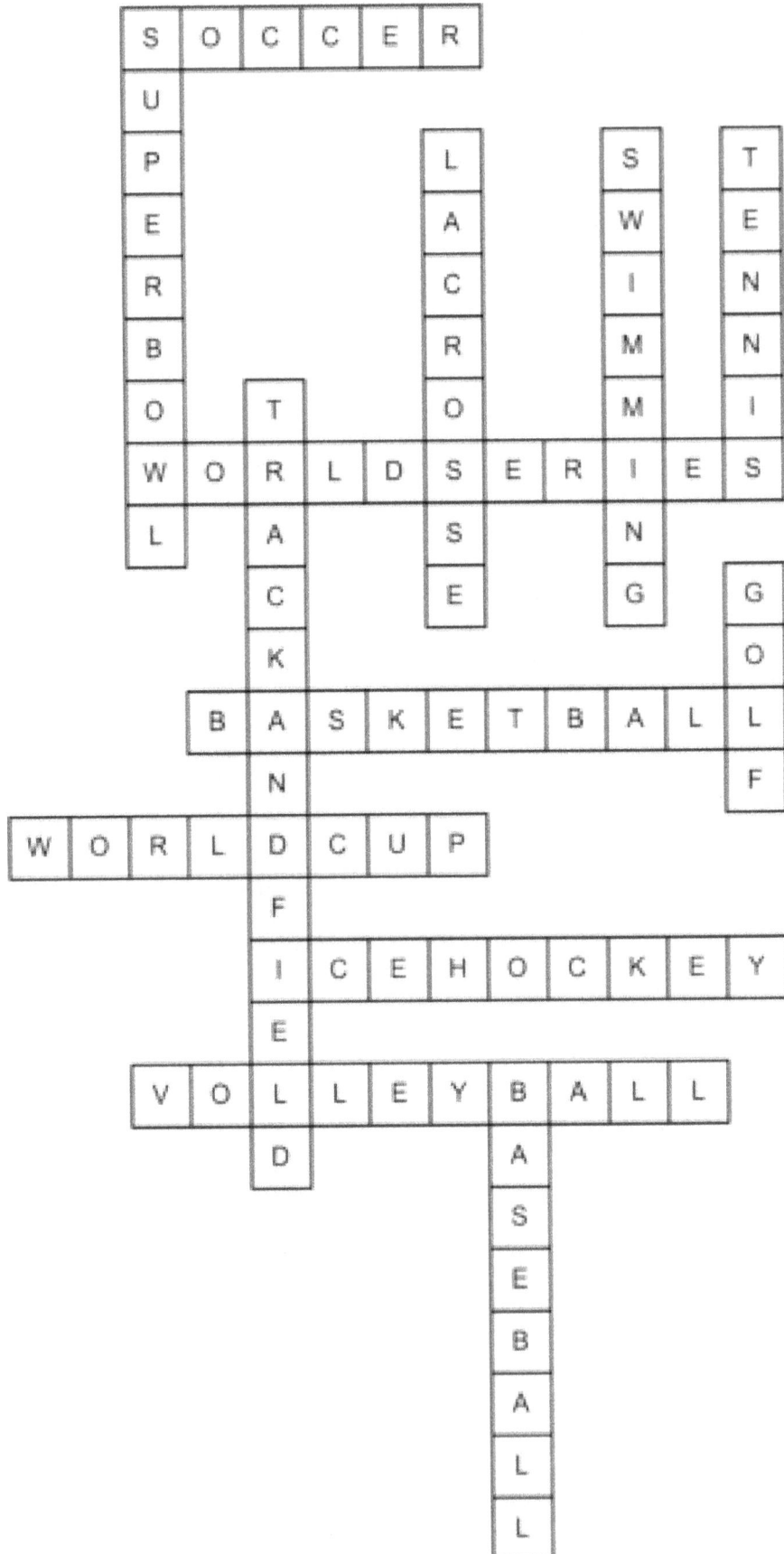

Sports

SOCCER

SUPERBOWL

LACROSSE

SWIMMING

TENNIS

WORLDSERIES

TRACKANDFIELD

BASKETBALL

GOLF

WORLDCUP

ICEHOCKEY

VOLLEYBALL

BASEBALL

Social Studies Crossword Puzzles: Grades 1–4

Transportation

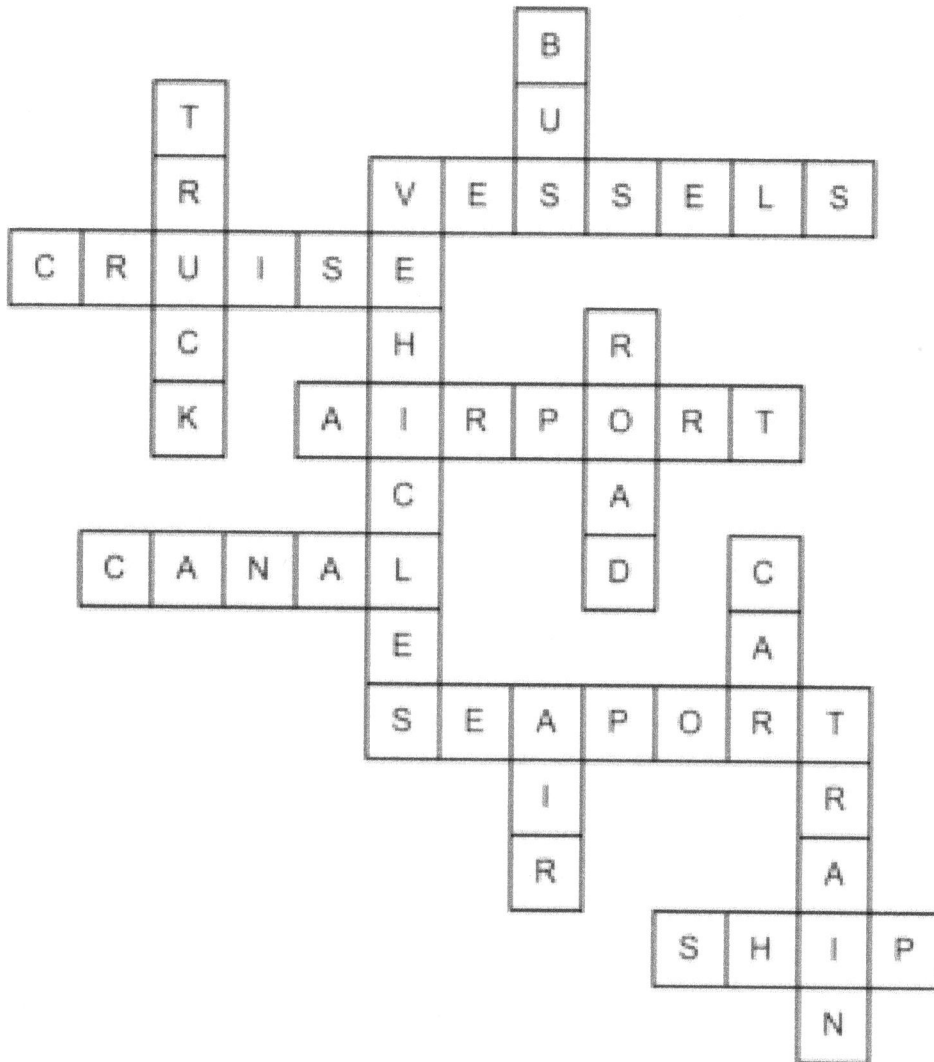

```
                          B
                          U
              V  E  S  S  E  L  S
        T     E
        R     H           R
C  R  U  I  S  E     A  I  R  P  O  R  T
        C     I              A
        K     C              D        C
              L                       A
     C  A  N  A  L                    A
              E                       T
              S  E  A  P  O  R  T     R
                    I                 A
                    R        S  H  I  P
                                      N
```

Colonial Life

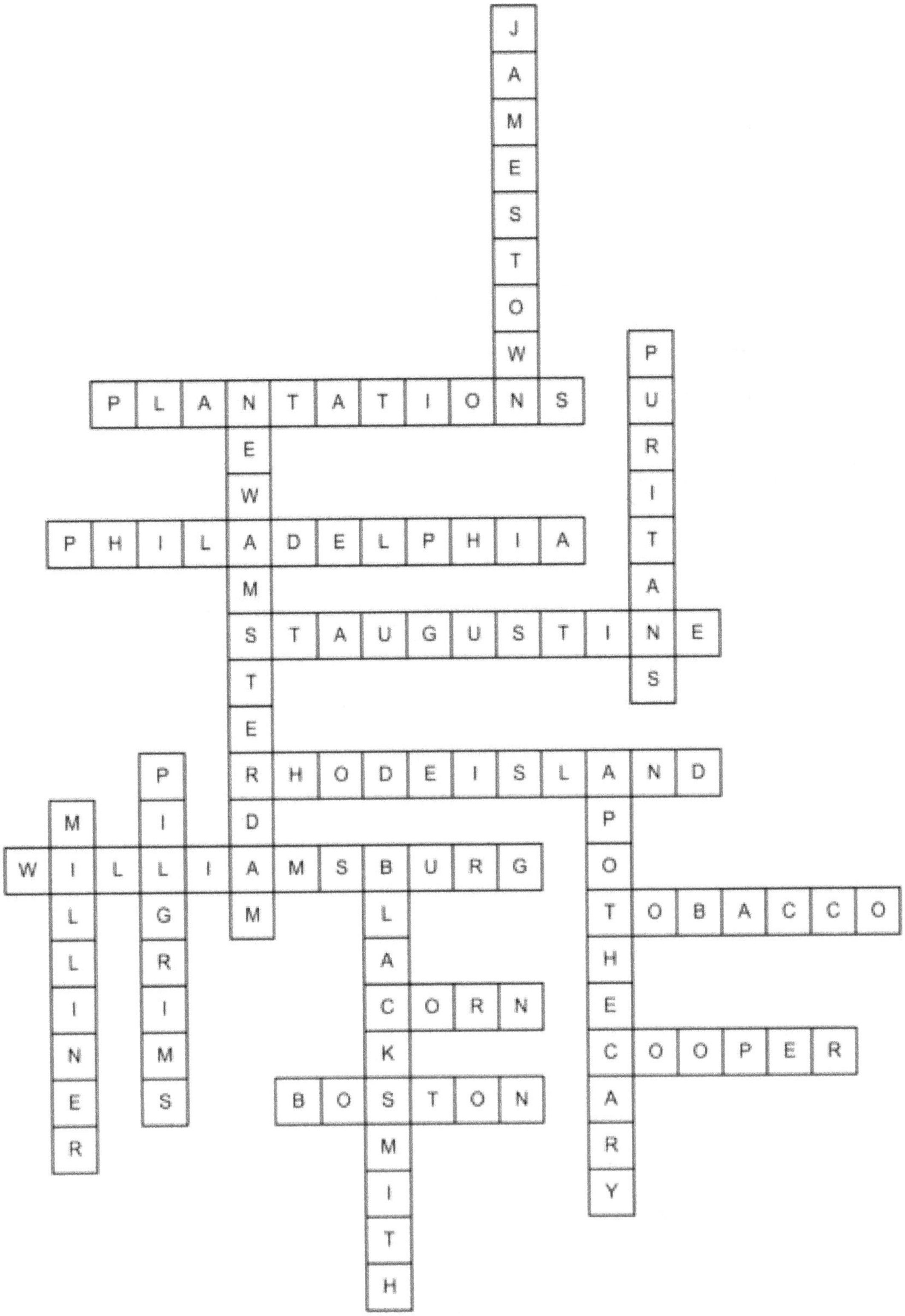
JAMESTOWN
PLANTATIONS
PURITANS
NEWAMSTERDAM
PHILADELPHIA
STAUGUSTINE
RHODEISLAND
PILGRIMS
MILLINER
WILLIAMSBURG
APOTHECARY
TOBACCO
BLACKSMITH
CORN
COOPER
BOSTON

Mixed Topics

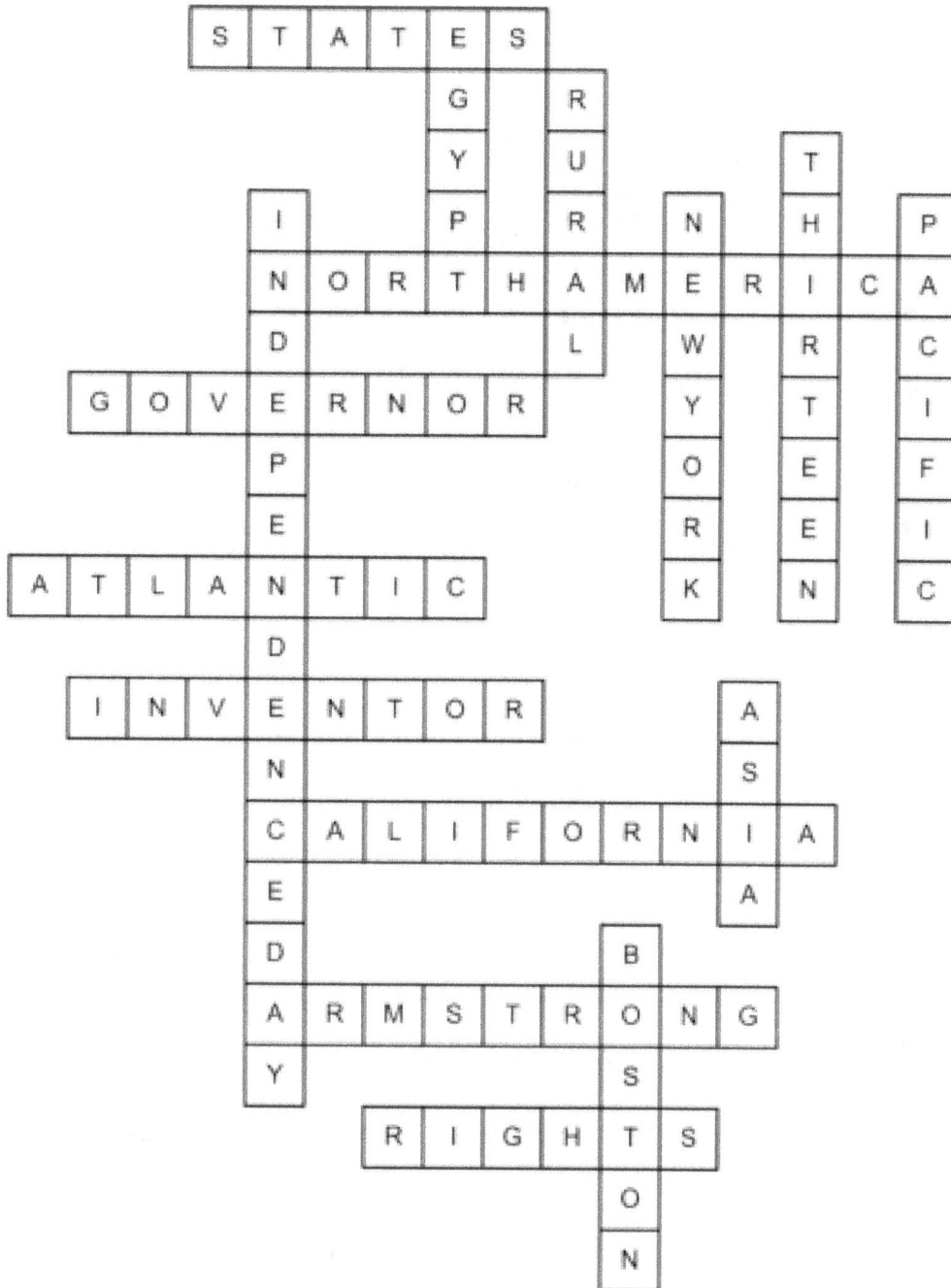

Social Studies Crossword Puzzles: Grades 1–4

Careers Word Search

	1	2	3	4	5	6	7	8	9	10	11	12	13	14	15	16
1	Q	M	L	O	L	M	L	D	P	U	R	A	P	H	E	V
2	A	V	P	L	X	K	X	L	E	X	V	O	D	V	C	A
3	V	A	Q	O	U	J	X	J	M	L	L	J	Q	N	Q	R
4	J	A	D	F	S	E	O	F	O	I	K	J	O	A	J	E
5	S	U	N	C	J	T	E	I	C	C	Y	S	R	I	H	T
6	D	V	L	E	E	M	A	E	G	B	B	I	E	R	U	H
7	E	F	W	V	Z	B	O	L	U	Q	X	M	K	A	R	G
8	N	Z	K	F	C	F	E	S	W	R	R	K	A	R	N	I
9	T	B	D	L	F	U	D	E	R	O	W	Z	B	B	R	F
10	I	H	J	I	M	R	M	J	Z	E	R	D	J	I	E	E
11	S	K	C	N	I	A	F	C	Z	N	M	K	I	L	T	R
12	T	E	I	V	U	R	E	Y	W	A	L	K	E	A	I	I
13	R	Y	E	F	O	R	R	E	B	R	A	B	K	R	A	F
14	H	R	W	S	M	S	S	E	R	T	I	A	W	Q	W	W
15	L	D	M	S	J	H	Y	E	Z	N	Q	D	G	P	E	T
16	N	R	O	Y	A	M	L	A	P	I	C	N	I	R	P	B

Word Search Answer/Hints

The words below are listed with their starting row and column.

BAKER 9:13

BARBER 13:12

BUS DRIVER 6:10

DENTIST 6:1

FIREFIGHTER 13:16

LAWYER 12:11

LIBRARIAN 11:14

MAYOR 16:6

NURSE 11:4

POLICE OFFICER 1:13

POSTAL WORKER 2:3

PRINCIPAL 16:15

WAITER 14:15

WAITRESS 14:13

Nations of the World Word Search

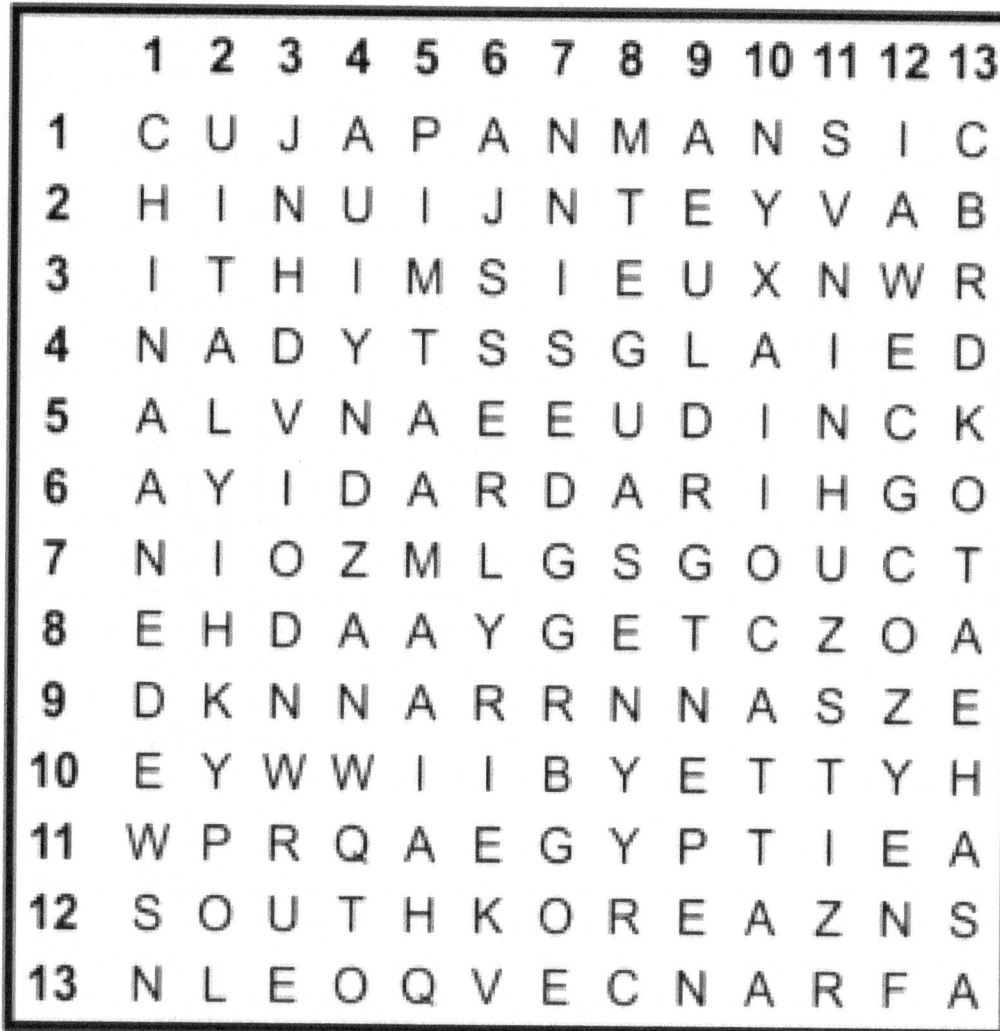

	1	2	3	4	5	6	7	8	9	10	11	12	13
1	C	U	J	A	P	A	N	M	A	N	S	I	C
2	H	I	N	U	I	J	N	T	E	Y	V	A	B
3	I	T	H	I	M	S	I	E	U	X	N	W	R
4	N	A	D	Y	T	S	S	G	L	A	I	E	D
5	A	L	V	N	A	E	E	U	D	I	N	C	K
6	A	Y	I	D	A	R	D	A	R	I	H	G	O
7	N	I	O	Z	M	L	G	S	G	O	U	C	T
8	E	H	D	A	A	Y	G	E	T	C	Z	O	A
9	D	K	N	N	A	R	R	N	A	S	Z	E	E
10	E	Y	W	W	I	I	B	Y	E	T	T	Y	H
11	W	P	R	Q	A	E	G	Y	P	T	I	E	A
12	S	O	U	T	H	K	O	R	E	A	Z	N	S
13	N	L	E	O	Q	V	E	C	N	A	R	F	A

Word Search Answer/Hints

The words below are listed with their starting row and column.

ARGENTINA 5:5	FRANCE 13:12	NIGERIA 5:11
BRAZIL 10:7	GERMANY 4:8	NORWAY 13:1
CANADA 1:13	INDIA 10:5	RUSSIA 6:9
CHILE 7:12	ITALY 2:2	SOUTH KOREA 12:1
CHINA 1:1	JAPAN 1:3	SWEDEN 12:1
EGYPT 11:6	KENYA 5:13	UNITED STATES 1:2
ENGLAND 10:9	MEXICO 1:8	

Anagrams

An anagram is a word, phrase, or name formed by rearranging the letters of another.

Example: POT and TOP

Use the clues to rearrange the letters of the given words to create anagrams.

1. RAW   WAR
CLUE: an armed conflict

2. VETO   VOTE
CLUE: what citizens do to choose a President

3. TASTE   STATE
CLUE: California, for example

4. PAINS   SPAIN
CLUE: a nation in Europe

5. MARY   ARMY
CLUE: an organized military force

6. HIPS   SHIP
CLUE: a means of transportation

7. MEAT   TEAM
CLUE: a group of people working together with common goal

8. KALE   LAKE
CLUE: a large body of water surrounded by land

9. AWL   LAW
CLUE: a rule of conduct

10. OILS   SOIL
CLUE: upper level of earth

Optional Lists of Words and Terms

These lists are provided for your convenience should you choose to use them.

Countries of the World

Argentina	Australia	Brazil	Canada	China
Egypt	England	France	Germany	Italy
Japan	Kenya	Mexico	Russia	

Communities

animals   bank   baseball   dentist   doctor
hospital   library   mail   police   restaurant   school
scouts   supermarket   teacher   worship

Families

aunt   brother   cousin   dad   grandfather
grandmother   mom   nephew   niece   parents
pet   sibling   sister   twins   uncle

Government

bill   cabinet   citizen   Congress   Constitution
democracy   election   executive   governor   judicial
laws   legislative   mayor   president   two   veto

Holidays and Symbols

Earth Day   Halloween   Independence   June   King
Liberty Bell   May   new year   Thanksgiving
valentine   veterans   Washington

       Social Studies Crossword Puzzles: Grades 1–4

Presidents

age   armed forces   citizen   executive   FDR
February   first lady   four   Jefferson   Lincoln
Madison   Obama   two   veto   Washington   White House

Sports

baseball   basketball   golf   ice hockey   lacrosse
soccer   Super Bowl   swimming   tennis
track and field   volleyball   World Cup   World Series

Transportation

air   airport   bus   canal   car   cruise
road   seaport   ship   train   truck
vehicles   vessels

Colonial Life

apothecary   blacksmith   Boston   cooper   corn   Jamestown
milliner   New Amsterdam   Philadelphia   Pilgrims   plantations
Puritans   Rhode Island   St. Augustine   tobacco   Williamsburg

Mixed Topics

Armstrong   Asia   Atlantic   Boston   California   Egypt
governor   Independence Day   inventor   New York
North America   Pacific   Rights   rural   states   thirteen